BURY ST. EDMUNDS

Photographed by John Curtis

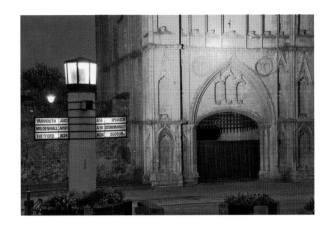

SALMON

INTRODUCTION

Bury St. Edmunds is a picturesque market town set in the heart of East Anglia. It grew up in Saxon times around the Great Abbey and for centuries, pilgrims from all over the world came here to the shrine of St. Edmund, the martyred King of East Anglia, who was the patron saint of England before the title passed to St. George. The Benedictine monks built a magnificent church to house the shrine and the monastery became one of the greatest religious establishments in the country.

The abbey was finally destroyed during the Dissolution of the Monasteries, and today the Abbey Gardens are a tranquil place much enjoyed by residents and visitors. Here the crumbling ruins of the Great Abbey stand in contrast to the grandeur of St. Edmundsbury Cathedral with its magnificent lantern tower and the splendid Parish Church of St. Mary's. The town also has historic connections with the Magna Carta. According to legend, the barons of England met here in 1214 and swore that they would force the king to accept the Charter of Liberties. These historic events are reflected in the town's coat of arms' Latin motto which translates as, *Shrine of a King, Cradle of the Law.*

Affectionately known as Bury, this gem of a town nestles in the beautiful Suffolk countryside. It was formerly the adminstrative centre of West Suffolk and a stroll through the narrow ancient streets, laid out in a grid pattern by the abbots, reveals a lovely mix of historic buildings, galleries, museums, weekly markets and shops, and cafés and restaurants.

Angel Hill

Athenaeum

It was at the Athenaeum, or Subscription Rooms, that Charles Dickens gave readings from his novels when he visited the town. It houses a fine chandeliered ballroom and there is a dome on the roof which once housed an observatory.

Abbot's Bridge

This ancient fortified bridge spans the River Lark on the eastern edge of Abbey Gardens. Part of the monastery boundary wall and dating from the 12th century, the bridge has three arches, each of which once contained a portcullis.

Abbey Church of St. Edmund

The sheer scale of the ruins of the Great Abbey Church leaves the visitor in no doubt of the power and the wealth once held by this Benedictine abbey. This was one of the largest Romanesque churches in Europe measuring more than 500 feet in length and 245 feet across. Originally built as a shrine to the martyred St. Edmund, the stone church replaced an earlier wooden structure in the early 11th century, but at the Dissolution of the Monasteries, the Great Abbey was dismantled and fell into ruin.

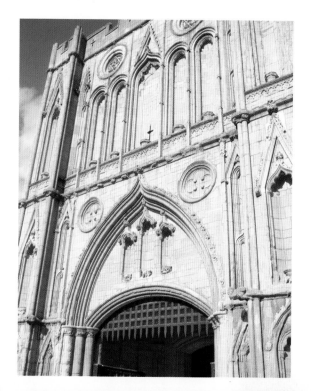

Great Gate

Violent riots broke out in the summer of 1327 when the townspeople stormed the Abbey and the original Abbey Gate was destroyed. A new gatehouse was built alongside it which stands proudly today at the entrance to the Abbey Gardens. This is one of several gatehouses which once stood along the boundary walls of the abbey precincts.

Great Churchyard

Between the Cathedral and St. Mary's Church is the vast space that is the Great Churchyard which still contains many ornate and carved tombstones and the remains of the 13th century Chapel of the Charnel. A tranquil timeless place, the Martyr's Memorial here remembers seventeen Protestant martyrs who were executed for their beliefs during the reign of Mary I.

St. Mary's Church

The splendour of the abbey precincts is further enhanced by St. Mary's Church, the third largest parish church in the country and built in the Perpendicular style in the early 15th century. In past times the western façade of the church served as the entrance for the townspeople, while the monks had their own separate entrance. Renowned for its magnificent hammer-beam angel roof, it is also the final resting place of Mary Rose Tudor, the sister of Henry VIII who became the Queen of France in 1514.

St. Edmundsbury Cathedral

The second church within the precincts of the former abbey, St. Edmundsbury is Suffolk's only cathedral. Originally the Parish Church of St. James, it was accorded cathedral status in 1914 and has been extended substantially over the years to present the imposing structure that greets us today. Changing the skyline of Bury forever, the central lantern tower is the most recent addition. The superb soaring Gothic-style tower was finally completed in 2005 – the crowning glory of this great Anglican cathedral.

St. Mary's Square

Lined by red-brick townhouses, fashionable St. Mary's Square was the location of the old horse market. In the early 1800s, the abolitionist Thomas Clarkson, who was a great friend of the poets Wordsworth and Coleridge, took up residence here. Clarkson also had good local connections as he was married to the daughter of William Buck, the founder of the Greene King Brewery.

Norman Tower

Abbot Anselm had the Norman Tower constructed between 1120 and 1148 with two functions in mind. It was to serve both as the grand main entrance to the abbey precincts and also as the bell tower for St. James's Church. Situated at the foot of Churchgate Street, the free-standing tower houses a fine peal of ten bells which were cast in 1785.

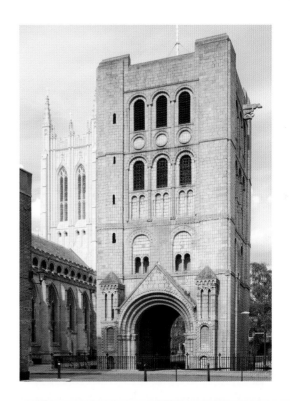

Greene King Brewery

The Greene King Brewery on Westgate Street was established in 1799 by the great grandfather of the writer Graham Greene at a time when many small brewhouses lined the street. The water used to brew the world famous beer still comes from an artesian well underneath the building and a museum and visitor shop next to the brewery traces the history and development of the company.

Theatre Royal

Another of Bury's familiar landmarks is the Theatre Royal just across the road from the brewery. A superb example of a Regency playhouse, the elegant little theatre has undergone major restoration work and reopened its doors to the public having been returned to its original 1819 configuration.

Unitarian Chapel

Along Churchgate stands this elegant chapel with its fine red-brick façade. Completed in 1712, the interior, with its central open space dominated by an ornate two-tiered pulpit and overlooked by original box pews in the galleries, remains largely unchanged. The chapel is an excellent venue for concerts, meetings and exhibitions.

Guildhall

A highly decorated 15th century porch leads into the old Guildhall. The historic building dates in part from the 13th century and has always played an important part in the history of the town, first as the home of the Guild of Merchants, then of the Candlemas Guild and later as the council chamber and the library.

Whiting Street

As an ancient market town, the centre of Bury still retains it medieval layout of narrow streets lined with listed buildings. One of the most picturesque streets is Whiting Street where this interesting group of cottages, formerly a single 'hall-house', can be found. The street was once the home of one of the earliest workhouses dating back to before 1621.

Corn Exchange

The grand front entrance of the Corn Exchange is a reminder of the importance of the town as a market centre. Carved figures representing agriculture look down from the decorative pediment above the imposing portico with its six Ionic columns.

The Nutshell

Until 2006 the smallest pub in the country, The Nutshell is a popular haunt in the heart of the town. Housed in a timber-framed Grade II listed building facing the Corn Exchange, it measures just 7 by 15 feet, though 102 customers managed to squeeze in here in a record-breaking attempt in 1984. On an average night, the pub welcomes a more moderate 20 people at a time.

Cupola House

Further along The Traverse, connected to The Nutshell by an underground passageway, is handsome Cupola House which today houses a restaurant. Named after the observatory on its steep roof-top, the elegant townhouse was built in 1693 for the local prosperous apothecary, Thomas Macro, who later went on to become Mayor of Bury.

Moyse's Hall Museum

The history of the Norman stone-and-flint building which today houses the Moyse's Hall Museum is long and fascinating. Thought to have been a tavern in medieval times, it was later used as the town gaol and workhouse, and from 1836 the police station. Finally in 1899, the museum, which traces the history of West Suffolk from prehistoric times to the present, opened to the public.

Market Cross and Boer War Memorial

Facing Moyse's Hall Museum on Cornhill is the Market Cross, which was the original corn exchange and designed by Robert Adam. In the centre of Cornhill stands a memorial commemorating the soldiers who gave their lives in the South African War of 1899-1902.

War Memorial

Facing Eastgate Street on Angel Hill, the War Memorial, constructed from Clipsham stone in the form of a Celtic cross, was erected in 1921 in honour of the men who fell in the First World War. The soldiers whose names are inscribed on the cross are also listed in the Book of Heroes which is kept in the cathedral.

Nearby, also on Angel Hill, is the unique 'Pillar of Salt' (illustrated on the title page), a modernistic illuminated road sign designed in 1935 and listed as a Grade II monument.

Nowton Park

On the outskirts of Bury is Nowton Park which comprises almost 200 acres of spectacular Suffolk countryside. The park was landscaped some 100 years ago giving it a typical Victorian feel with a grand lime avenue, a walled garden, a folly, ponds and luscious meadows rich in wildlife and flowers.

Pakenham Windmill

The village of Pakenham to the east of Bury is unique in having both a windmill and a watermill in full working order. The superb restored brick tower mill, which has been in the ownership of the Bryant family for the past 100 years, stands on a hilltop in Thieves Lane presenting a magnificent sight with its black-tarred brickwork and white cap.

Pakenham Watermill

There has been a watermill on this site overlooking the River Blackbourne since at least 1086. The handsome watermill is today owned by the Suffolk Building Preservation Trust and produces traditional stone-ground wholemeal flour from locally grown wheat.

West Stow Anglo-Saxon Village
Using only contemporary tools and techniques, part of an early Anglo-Saxon village has been re-created at West Stow. Beneath the Breckland sands almost 70 houses and many other structures have been uncovered.

Ickworth House
Flanked by two grand wings, the giant rotunda at Ickworth House was the brainchild of the eccentric 4th Earl of Bristol. The unusual Italianate country house has wonderful collections of paintings, furniture and Georgian silver.

The Rose Garden

The tranquillity of the Abbey Gardens offers a delightful bolt-hole in the middle of the hustle and bustle of the busy market town. The glorious cathedral is complemented by the beautiful Old English Rose Garden dedicated to the American servicemen stationed here during the Second World War.

Published by J. Salmon Ltd.,
Sevenoaks, Kent TN13 1BB. © 2008
Website: www.jsalmon.co.uk Telephone: 01732 452381.
Email: enquiries@jsalmon.co.uk.

Design and photographs by John Curtis © John Curtis.

Pictures: p.16 courtesy of the Theatre Royal/National Trust and p.30 courtesy of St. Edmundsbury Borough Council/ West Stow Anglo-Saxon Village Trust.

Printed in China.

ISBN 978-1-84640-126-8
Title page photograph: 1930's road sign, Angel Hill.
Half title page: Angel Hill
Front cover photograph: Cathedral and Abbey Gardens.
Back cover photograph: St. Edmund Statue.

First Impression 2008
Second Impression 2010

Salmon Books

ENGLISH IMAGES SERIES

Photography by John Curtis

Titles available in this series

English Abbeys and Priories

English Gardens

English Country Towns

English Cottages

English Landscape Gardens

English Follies

English Villages

English Country Pubs

English Castles

English Cathedrals

English Country Churches

Jane Austen's England

Romantic England

Mysterious England